THE ROLE OF AN INTERCESSOR

Lovella Mogere & Collaborative

Nous Mass Media products are available at special quantity discounts for bulk purchase for sales promotions, premiums, fund-raising, and educational needs. For details, email Nous Mass Media at nousmassmedia@gmail.com, website: https://bit.ly/36eoN9M or call 832-598-8608.

The Role of An Intercessor Vol III - "The Eyes of The Revelator" by Lovella Mogere and Collaborative, Nous Mass Media.

Chief Editor: The Write Legacy LLC, www.thewritelegacy.com.

ISBN: 97-98573089423

Contents

The Eyes of the Revelator **5**

The Seer Sees with Spiritual Eyes **10**

You're Not Crazy! **18**

My Father's Eyes **27**

Trust What You See **37**

Mantled for the Assignment **45**

Seer Look Up **53**

The Birther Within **61**

A Dreamer's Call To Prayer **81**

Dedication

To the Eyes of the Revelator" the Revealing Prophets, the Seers, that have the ability to see into dimensions. Your prophetic graces operate outside the dimension of time. You see into events of the time with precision and accuracy. The Eyes of the Revelator see, hear and witness heavenly activities, engage angelic beings and operate at a high level of the word of knowledge. Now and again, the Lord will trans relocate you, Seer, into supernatural realms for you to see what He has for His people. When the Lord allows this, you see what has never been revealed because you prophetically flow outside time constraint. Seers can flow between dimensions. They have a precise predictive gift fore they have seen it unfold in the supernatural realms. The Eyes of the Revelator only sees, hears and feels when the Lord gives him/her access to. You are #TheEyesOf TheRevelator.

Dr. Lovella Mogere

1

The Eyes of the Revelator

By Lovella Mogere

The next wave of God Is going to be disruptive, It will involve a redefinition of the church, apostolic centers, micro churches and ministries that are redefining the next move in the body of Christ. This movement is going to challenge the traditional control of ecclesiastical structures and the mental models of projection of the functionality of how the church should be. With an overriding of languages the descriptive wavelengths of frequencies that have flat-lined over time, one have to be mindful not to resurrect dead pulses or continuum moves of God, that has come to the end of its fulfillment, for the greater expression of the Glory of God.

Who are the Eyes of the Revelators?

The eyes of the revelators are the seer's, who are at the end of the age (end-time), that have the power to taste the age, see the time to come liken to King David. David saw the future, he was given access to bring the future into his present. Amos 9:13 states "The days are coming," declares the LORD, "when the reaper will be overtaken by the plowman and the planter by the one treading grapes. New wine will drip from the mountains and flow from all the hills. What does that mean? It means, with higher levels of seers and prophetic leadership in place they can confirm what they saw and call in into this era now.

The Revelators – reveals the legal declaration of God's intent in the earth realm. When I speak of the eyes of the revelator, I speak of God's prophetic perspective, giving the height and depth of the interpretation of God's consciousness. Amos 3:7 states "Surely the Lord will do nothing, but he revealeth his secret unto his servants the prophets".

God gave David the *tabniyth translated in* Greek and Hebrew for plan, form, construction and design. 1 Chronicles 28:19, David states precisely that God gave this information to him "by the spirit" (verse 12) and "in writing by His hand the works of this pattern" (verse 19). David got into a place in worship where he saw our day and had the authority to release time in his day. He saw the plan and blueprint of the temple in the future and brought a jurisdiction *(the official power to make legal decisions and judgments)* from the future into his era to build the temple, in which he was able to listen to prophetic counsel with prophetic worship and the utterance that do with it.

How did David do it?

This is remarkable! 1 Chronicles 28:19, David states precisely that God gave this information to him "by the spirit" (verse 12) and "in writing by His hand the works of this pattern" (verse 19). David did it by executing spiritual strategies given, he had to go in the spirit and make tangible what he saw. He did something about what he saw. "All this," David said, "I have in writing as a result of the LORD's hand on me, and he enabled me to understand all the details of the plan."

David's Desire and His Command to Solomon

David greatly desired and intended to build the Temple, but God prevented him from doing so because he was "a man of war, and has shed blood" (1 Chronicles 28:3). David, therefore, gathered all the necessary materials together for the construction of the Temple. When David was near death he had Solomon, Prince and Heir to the throne (chosen by God, 1 Chronicles 28:5 and 29:1), brought before him with the people of Israel attending. All were to be told important information concerning the construction of the Temple that God would allow Solomon to build. "And you, Solomon my son, take heed now; for the Lord hath chosen you to build a house for the sanctuary: be strong, and do it." 1 Chronicles 28:9–10.

So you know? David expanded the real estate of Israel 400 per cent more than Saul because he didn't do it by the edge of the sword he did it by implementing spiritual strategies that came out of seeing the future. We're talking about a radical accelerator. David went into the natural and implemented what was given in the spirit.

You, the Eyes of the Revelator" the Revealing Prophets, the Seers, that have the ability to see into dimensions. Your prophetic graces operate outside the dimension of time. You see into events of the time with precision and accuracy. The Eyes of the Revelator see, hear and witness heavenly activities, engage angelic beings and operate at a high level of the word of knowledge. Every now and again, the Lord will trans relocate you, Seer, into supernatural realms for you to see what He has for His people. When the Lord allows this, you see what has never been revealed because you prophetically flow outside time constraint. Seers can flow between dimensions. They have a precise predictive gift fore they have seen it unfold in the supernatural realms. The Eyes of the Revelator only sees, hears and feels when the Lord gives him/her access to. You are #TheEyesOf TheRevelator.

About the author

Dr. Lovella Mogere, is an entrepreneur, #1 best-selling author and motivational speaker. She empowers women globally to live life intentionally by tapping into the power of intentional thinking. To learn more about Dr. Mogere visit www.lovellamogere.com.

2

The Seer Sees with Spiritual Eyes

By Danielle Kennedy

The Seer sees with spiritual eyes, visions, pictures, or scenes in the mind's eye, dreams, or even with one's natural eye. They interpret, clarify eternal truth, foresee the future from the past and the present. Another name used for a seer is a prophet. A teacher of known truth as a seer is a perceiver of hidden truth, and a revelator is a bearer of new truth. Perceivers become aware of things or events through senses or, as we like to call it, intuition. A Revelator is one that reveals the will of God.

As a child born with spiritual gifts, you are often met with identity crisis symptoms because you just don't fit the puzzle. Not understanding who, what, or why you are the way you are and hearing things differently from others. Even your movement is different from those around you. You're not able to fully relate or identify with your loved ones either. I can remember growing up seeing things that I didn't understand. Some things will make you appear crazy to others, but to you, it's as real as hearing a voice speaking to you about what you're seeing. You begin to speak what the voice is saying, and those around question the source of your knowledge. They'd be taken aback, asking, "Who told you that?" and I would call it the big voice until I understood that the voice that I was hearing was God, the Father himself, speaking to me.

There were many things shown to me, some good, some bad. I can remember a dream that I had about my cousin, who was younger than me, and all the events that led up to her demise. I can smell, hear, and move about as if I was there, I tried to warn her of what I saw in my dream, but she didn't take it seriously. God let me see that everyone she was in opposition with, she made peace with them. I talked to her one last time before the weekend of her girls' trip, and I told her to have fun but be careful. Her last words to me were, "cousin, I'm not afraid to die." That Sunday, she died, and that shook me to the very depths of my soul. Her death wasn't the first or the last that I dreamt of. There were many more I had experienced.

Some of the good things I experienced were someone or even strangers being blessed with many gifts of job promotions, new homes, blessings of wealth, etc. I could remember God saying to me pay attention to everything in the dream or vision, as I would see in passing. When it came back around, it felt like what we call Deja vu, meaning I've seen this before. Not all dreams and visions are bad, but when you don't understand your gift, it can make you feel like it's a curse. I was so confused about who I was and why I was chosen for this gift—feeling misunderstood, looked upon as weird, crazy or people just being plain scared of me. Things got better as time went on, and I felt that God knew that it was a lot for me to handle, but the gift never left me. I would always be told that I have an unusual anointing or gift on my life. I would always say to myself, what does that mean? So, I sought God on what and why I do the things that I do. God began to show me in his word about prophets in the Bible that spoke of how God the Father uses them to speak his word. He also gave them dreams or visions and interpretations of those dreams or visions. One scripture was 1st Samuel 9:9; it shows that many were led to Seers to get messages or dreams or visions interpreted from God's chosen vessels. I read about God using his people to demonstrate his miracles, signs, and wonders. For God's word says to study to show myself approved that everything we go through in life is in God's word, which is the blueprint of life that shows you where you are and what to do as well with and without God.

Job is one of my favorite books of the Bible. It taught me how to get through many tests and trials as well as pain and hurt. Although he went through all the suffering, he never turned his back on God, and he was firm in his belief in the Father. I can relate to Job's experiences because of my pain and hurt of those physical afflictions that can take a toll on your body and leave you with sickness. I can truly say that without God, I would not have made it out.

As a Seer, you see the good, the bad, and the ugly. The warning comes before destruction, and God would always alert me when an attack was coming. He would always say, get in your stance, and he would begin to show me in the spirit what strategy to take on the field of warfare. It's important to be in the right position before the attack begins. What was it like? I'm glad you asked. It was like an inner-outer body experience. I could feel God before me, see myself and hear the voice of God asking me, "Do you trust me?" I answered, "Yes, I do." He said, "Don't be afraid, for I am with you. Move when I say move, speak when I say speak." I watched the Holy Spirit's words that were spoken through me slowly take power away from the spirit to the point of surrendering, and the Words of God cast it back to the pits of hell from which it came. The spirit had to be replaced with one of God's spirits; my favorite is love because no matter what, love will always cause a person not to be angry. Spirits are sent to attack what God placed inside of you. It comes to rob you of your true identity in God the Father. Were there many more? Yes, and there are more to come.

Life is a battlefield, and I have experienced this in churches, family gatherings, work, and even my home life. Spiritual battles can be very draining of your energy and strength. This is why you have to stay covered in prayer, reading your word, and staying in the presence of God. You have to have an intimate relationship with God, the Father, for the strength to get through each battle. I learned that the higher the calling on your life, the greater the warfare is. This walk can be very uncomfortable and lonely but very rewarding at the same time. By being obedient to his will and whatever he asked of you. He has already made provisions no matter what the circumstances. So, you can't worry about what people might say or do. Stay focused on the assignment and see it through because some will embrace, and some won't. Again, it's by your own free will, and in this, I found that surrendering to God's will and my gift will allow God to teach me how to flow and operate in Him through this life journey. When I learned that, I was able to embrace the new me in Christ. By walking fully in my gifting and using myself as a living walking testament of who God is in and through my life, His agape love shown through me gives others hope and assurance in this battle that we go through. You will never be alone, love conquerors all so if you're ever in doubt about who you are in Christ Jesus, as the word says, "Seek ye the kingdom of God first, and all shall be added; knock, and the door shall be answered, ask and it shall be given." Everything is at the tips of your fingers; it's just a matter of applying yourself and studying the word of God so you will come to know your true identity in the Kingdom of God. Be blessed.

About the author

Danielle Kennedy is a loving mother of one daughter, a God-given son, and the grandmother of one beautiful granddaughter who has devoted her life, gifts, and talents to motivate, inspire and arouse the body of Christ to worship God in spirit and truth. She has many years of service in evangelism, children's ministry, and also prison ministry. Danielle uses testimonies to uplift and encourages the people of God that there is life after pain if we just let go and let God.

Contact Info:

Email: teepot229@gmail.com

https://www.facebook.com/danielle.wells.3910

3

You're Not Crazy!

By Tahkyra TK Terrell

I remember attending the University of Michigan, being on the bus thinking to myself: "Lord, please shut my eyes! I don't want to see anymore." I thought I was losing my mind. It was my junior year, and I was on my way to a work-study position. On that bus, I saw faces shifting. I saw people looking gray and ashen; some students looked bright and illuminated. I saw monsters in their faces. I was looking in the mirror and saw my face shifting and distorting at times. I thought that I was undergoing some form of a psychotic break. Especially as a psychology major, I thought I knew what was happening at that time. The truth was that I wasn't having a psychotic break. I was undergoing spiritual transformation, and God was increasing my discernment. I didn't have access to that information. I was unaware of the necessary knowledge to embrace the gift that God was showing me. It would be years later before God opened my eyes again to that magnitude.

When I was first asked to participate in this book, I thought and asked God what I have to say? The first memory I had was that period of time in my life. Then I heard the words, "You're not crazy!" They echoed and resounded in my ear over the next few days. "You're not crazy!" Throughout my life, I believed the lie that I was weird. Peculiar and crazy, if you will. I thought that something was inherently wrong with me when I'd dream things that took place before they happened. I thought that there was something wrong with me when I would "zone out" and see things that others didn't see.

Was I Bipolar, a manic? Was I schizophrenic and having paranoid delusions?

As a Prophetic Seer, I believe the biggest challenge you will have to face is yourself—your thoughts. Your beliefs are about who you are, what you believe about God, what you believe about who God thinks you are, and the truth is somewhere in there. My logic behind this is that we all filter life and perceptions through the lens of our experience. As a mental health therapist, I see this daily. If my perception is negative, dysfunctional, or maladaptive, then how I view life and experiences will be filtered through those negative perceptions. I firmly believe that it is important to focus on our metacognition, a term that means to think about our thinking. It's not important to solely think about our thoughts' content, but we have to think of the context in which we think our thoughts. We have to be just as diligent in thinking about the "how" of how we think about things.

Let's take a look at Saul as he was on his way to Damascus. If you know the Bible, in Acts 9, verses 1-9, there is an account where Saul is on his way to do what he believes is the right thing: persecute and arrest new converts and followers of the Way, followers of Christ. He had a vision, heard an audible voice ask, "Why are you persecuting me?"

Everyone with Saul heard the voice, but they didn't see anyone there. Saul was the only one who saw the Lord at that moment. He then went blind and isolated himself for weeks. Later in chapter 9, the Lord instructed a man named Ananias to baptize and pray for Saul, which then caused scales to be removed from his eyes. We now know the account of the transformation of Saul to Apostle Paul.

What is amazing in this is that although God orchestrated the entire situation, it was the revelation of Christ that Saul had to accept the position himself for the scales to be removed from his eyes. His vision and his sight had to change. The scales simply fell off, and

Saul regained his vision. Why is this important Tahkyra? Here's why: Saul was with a group of people who heard the same thing he did but couldn't see what he saw. Let's not forget that Saul was a teacher of the law. He knew the law's content, but his perception, vision, and sight were filtered through his experiences and position as a teacher. His beliefs and convictions were in alignment with what he was taught; until that encounter with Jesus. Sometimes, God will give us a revelation that not everyone will have access to. God will speak things to you through the lens of your experiences. He will show you things that not everyone will have the capacity to understand. Not your spouse, family, friends, pastor, even mentors! And you have to be okay with that! You have to be okay with the fact that you will walk alone on this journey at times. You will see things that you don't want to see. God will show you things that will leave your mouth wide open!

I had to learn and challenge myself to believe that just like God chose Saul on the road to Damascus-He chose me too. Your experience is your experience.

No one has lived your life, but you. What has to fall off our eyes are the unhealed experiences that make us think we are crazy, which means traumatic, painful things that only God can touch. Every time you even utter the phrase "I'm crazy," it's a verbal contract with the enemy and yourself to keep you in bondage. We have got to be cautious of our thoughts and what we are thinking. What we think filters what we see. 2 Corinthians 10:5 (NIV) says, "5 We demolish arguments and every pretension that sets itself up against the knowledge of God, and we take captive every thought to make it obedient to Christ." What we have to understand is we have to be healed in our thought life, the content and context of our thoughts, as a way to demolish the arguments and pretensions that go against the knowledge of God. What do I mean? I mean that we can't be so spiritual that we neglect healing the wounds that can take place in our soul. It's about balance. Things have happened in our lives that shape our perceptions, sights, and just like Paul, we can be doing what we believe is right and end up going against the knowledge of God. It causes us to paint prophecies and see visions from our soul's wounds and not see from the realm of the spirit.

That is why it is critical to challenge that thought and say, "I am not crazy." As a Seer, God will have a greater capacity to use you when your thoughts line up with what He says about you when your thoughts are in alignment with the content and context of what God has said about your experiences. The revelation of Christ that came to Saul, now Paul, went beyond his experiences, what he was taught, and what he thought he was doing right. It came from the vision and revelation of who Christ is and said that Saul was. It opened His eyes beyond the historical data stored in his mind.

Are you willing to stretch and grow beyond what is comfortable in your thoughts, perceptions, in the plans and visions that God can and will download to you? When God opened my eyes again, I had to go through a lot of personal growth and healing. If you remember, I also said that I saw some distortions of myself when I looked in the mirror at that time. Now, I have a support system. Now, I am ready, open, and teachable-even when it is beyond my comfort zone. Now, I accept the days when I am alone on the journey. It's not easy, but had I not done the work to operate from proper spiritual alignment and challenge the thought of being crazy, my capacity would have been limited to my past experiences. I would be operating from old perceptions that wouldn't be able to stretch, like new wine in old wineskins.

I believe that God is opening the eyes of many just as the prophet Joel said, "It shall come about after this that I shall pour out My Spirit on all mankind, And your sons and your daughters will prophesy, your old men will dream dreams, your young men will see visions." (Joel 2:28 AMP). To be both effective, proficient, and efficient, whether it is your office or your gift as a seer and revelator, you have to make sure that you have done the work to bring into alignment your thoughts of yourself and God's thoughts of you!

Acceptance is key. How can you trust yourself, trust God even if you don't accept it? You aren't crazy! It's just how God wired you!

About the author

Tahkyra T. Terrell is a native of Detroit, MI. After graduating from the University of Michigan and then Ashland Theological Seminary, she became a licensed clinical therapist. As she worked with clients with intense trauma and addictions, she had noticed that there was often a disconnection between what one can think and what one can feel. She reflected over her own personal recovery from traumatic experiences that had been normalized because of growing up in the inner city, strict family values, and even from experiences in the church. She noticed her own disconnection between the relationship she had with God, the relationship with herself, and between her thoughts and what she felt. Personal integration took place by incorporating both therapeutic and biblical concepts. Through the power of reclaiming personal experiences, there is power in connecting to the stories of our past and what we believe about ourselves. We can change what we believe as we get to know ourselves beyond the lens of what happened to us. Tahkyra hopes to assist others to grow in the relationship with themselves, with God, and bridge the gap between biblical and therapeutic concepts to bring healing from painful experiences.

Email: tahkyraterrell01@gmail.com

Facebook: https://www.facebook.com/tahkyra.terrell

4

My Father's Eyes

By Quentina M. Attipoe

As an Intercessor and a beloved daughter of the Most High, my prayer has always been to have the eyes of my Heavenly Father. I recall Amy Grant singing a song entitled, "Father's Eyes". The lyrics, particularly the chorus, resonates with me until this day. CHORUS:

She's got her father's eyes,

Her father's eyes;

Eyes that find the good in things,

When good is not around;

Eyes that find the source of help,

When help just can't be found;

Eyes full of compassion,

Seeing every pain;

Knowing what you're going through

And feeling it the same.

Just like my father's eyes,

My father's eyes,

My father's eyes,

Just like my father's eyes.

For those who are not spiritually-minded, the lyrics may seem to be of a girl whose eyes resemble that of her earthly father. However, for those who walk in the spirit, who worship in spirit and truth... it is humbling to have the eyes of my Heaven Father. The Father's eyes look past the situation into the individual's spirit or the spirit behind the matter. In Samuel 16:7, The Lord told Samuel that man looks on the outer while He looks at the heart. When an intercessor has the eyes of the Father, their sight comes from the place of identity, which is seated in Christ. The perception as a seer is filtered through personal experiences with Christ.

As with many, I could "see" in the spirit the majority of my life. Until the seer's ability becomes mature and developed, it is not often recognized and dismissed, especially in children. Whether in dreams, experiencing a sense of déjà vu, or seeing situations before me like puzzles, my experience as an intercessor and seer has developed. That development occurred in the secret place.

It is where intimacy grows and where the seer first encounters the presence of Jesus. Just as Jesus healed the eyes of the blind, it is in the secret place with him that healing of wounds and trauma first occurs in the intercessor. As the intimacy between the intercessor and Abba Father deepens, the vision to see develops. It is from the secret place that the seer emerges. Always aware of the Holy Spirit's presence, the seer exchanges natural sight for the sight of the Father.

SIGHT... SEEING... VISION...

Growing in faith and maturity, I have learned that what occurs in the natural reflects spiritual truth.

A military marksman becomes proficient at choosing an elevated and secure location. When in position, the marksman looks through the "sight" of his weapon to gives him exponential power and focus on hitting the intended target accurately. The marksman will identify and diligently study the target and environment carefully to ensure that he is "seeing" the target accurately and not aiming amiss. Based on his experience and time spent studying, the marksman may perceive where to look or focus. This is not much different from a hunter in a tree stand, who studies the area and waits, listens, and watches for the target.

Lastly, a marksman will adjust his "sight" and aim to focus on his "vision."

Sight, or power to see, depends on your location. The strategy of the intercessor is dependent on the position of being seated with the Father. The sight of an intercessor, or a seer, is no different. When you become seated with the Father, you begin to see as He sees. My question to you is, where are you seated? Psalm 23:5 tells us that there is a table set for us. Many have not received the revelation that they are even worthy of sitting at the table. At the same time, others have the revelation but are not sure where they are seated at the table. Are you seated at the table? If so, where are you seated?

Some picture themselves far from Abba seated at the "kiddie table." They feel unworthy or do not believe that they have the authority of others. Maybe it is simply that they do not understand their authority. Others see themselves at the end of the table or somewhere in the middle of the table. They have the right to be at the table but not the authority or importance as spiritual leaders. The beloved sees themselves as next to the Father and from the vantage point of Jesus.

Your position at the table is solely based on your relationship with the Father. Position determines your intimacy. Your intimacy develops your gift as a seer. To see as the Father sees, first, you must become aware of your proximity to him. He is in you, as you are in Him—one with each other as you see through His eyes. You must believe that you are worthy of having the vision and sight that you were created to have. For many, this is a new paradigm, a way of thinking. We have believed ourselves to be less than who we were created to be. Our belief has clouded our vision. To see clearly, we must "cleanse the lens" through which we are looking. The lens is only cleansed through the love of the Father, the love of Jesus.

Seeing depends on where you are actively looking or what you are perceiving. Hebrews 11:1 tells us, "Now faith is the substance of things hoped for and the evidence of things not seen." The seer is graced to actively look into the realm of what is not seen with the physical eye. Without the restriction of time or space, the seer may look into past, present, or future events related to the individual for which she is praying. John the Beloved, who was also the Revelator, saw Heaven and visions of the end of days. Vision, or the ability to see, think, or plan, depends on your eyes' condition. To see physically requires the eye's organ and the nerves to transmit information regarding the light, reflections, and refractions of the light received. To see spiritually is also the reception of light, the Holy Spirit's light, the light of Jesus.

Throughout the Bible, the heart of the Father was revealed to the seer. Many times, the vision of the seer needed to be adjusted. Abraham's ability to understand and receive the revelation of his covenant came as he looked at the stars. Elisha's servant's eye had to be opened to see the protection of the host of heaven rather than the enemy before them.

As the saying goes, "with great power comes great responsibility." Responsibility to pray and cover is a great one. Many want to know how to see or understand what they see in visions or dreams. Few inquire about the responsibility of the seer. The life of a seer is sacrificial and often misunderstood. Yet, it is full of excitement, never knowing who or what will be revealed. The seer becomes the protector of all the Holy Spirit is revealing. Others often misunderstand the resulting quietness or watching of the people and things in my atmosphere as arrogance or anger. Often what is seen is not to be repeated, but prayer points to intercede and cover the individual, leader, or region.

The revelation of being a seer and understanding the gift within me has allowed me to intercede for others in powerful ways. The revelation shared by the Holy Spirit's intimacy begins a new level of trust between you and The Father. A trust filled with child-like faith, with eyes full of wonder and amazement. Jesus said to "come to the Father as a little child." As I open my mind to the wonders and majesty of my Creator, my Father, and my Lord, I am not restricted to accepting things that I see but open to new realm and possibilities.

The more I come into the realization that Abba created me to be one with Him and in His image, the more the Spirit realm opens to me. The more I exist daily between the natural realm and the spiritual realm and seek His wisdom.

The more I seek the wisdom of my Abba Father, the more the eyes of my heart are opened...

The more the eyes of my heart open to my Abba's love, the more I grow in His love...

The more I grow the love of my Abba Father, the more He reveals to me!

About the Author

Quentina Maria Attipoe is a beloved daughter of our Most High God, cherished wife, and blessed mother of a blended family. In partnership with the Lord, she and her husband, Edmond, co-founded AGAPE Ghana in

2019, a ministry that provides individual and family assistance with access to medical, social, and educational services in Ghana. In 2020, AGAPE Worldwide, Inc. was established to expand assistance to other nations and is currently assisting a children's home in Uganda.

Contact Info:

Quentina Attipoe

QMPJAttipoe@outlook.com

Facebook: Quentina Attipoe, Author

AGAPE Worldwide/AGAPE Ghana

Missions for the 21st Century

http://agapeghana.org

AGAPEGhana@outlook.com

info@agapeghana.org

Facebook: AGAPE Ghana

5

Trust What You See

By Sean Hunter

As I begin to write, excitement and revelation begin to bubble up in me. It thrills me to unpack and unfold my journey as a seer that is called to intercession. There are highs and lows as an intercessor but do not worry; your helper is on the inside of you, and he will help advance you. Connect with your partner (Holy Spirit) so the will of the Father can be done. As you read, I pray that you will gather information from the highlights of my journey and trust who you are.

It all started at a place where I was broken, and life was crushing me—reliving the process of an olive being pressed for the substances it holds. Through that process, I discovered the power of prayer. In October 2015, God's Spirit began drawing me back to Christ. I knew it was urgent, so urgent that not surrendering to this call would cause my life to be cut short. In the first two or three months of my journey, I battled with past heartaches and pains. Those battles were both spiritual and emotional. During the two- or three-months process, I started dreaming intensely. Every time I closed my eyes, I would see. It was a supernatural journey. In the beginning, most of my dreams were horrific and dreadful. Most of the dreams were demonic attacks. Mentally it was too much, I did not want to deal with those types of dreams, but it was necessary to go through that process. It gave me strength and birthed my newfound love for prayer. It came to a point in my life that I just felt a thirst to pray and not just to pray for myself. It was a burden to pray for others. Prayer took me on a journey in the spirit, allowing me to see like never before. What once seemed like too much strengthened me. My momentum heightened. I began praying three to four times a day. As time went on, I started experiencing supernatural visions that had me desiring to see more. Feeling like it was just my imagination, but it kept constantly happening. Through my obedience, I began to see still and motion pictures in my mind. It would appear, and I began to realize that it was God opening my spiritual eyes. Through that stage of testing, I felt like Jeremiah the Prophet when God taught him on his ability to see in the spirit. "Moreover, the word of the Lord came unto me, saying, Jeremiah, what seest thou? And I said, I see a rod of an almond tree. Then said the Lord unto me, thou hast well seen for I will hasten my word to perform it." Jeremiah 1:11-12 KJV.

As those tests from the Lord increased, my prayer of intercession became more effective. When you pray, what you see is such an advantage. Can you imagine having the password to someone's bank account that has access to millions? I call that a spiritual jackpot. Being a seer that's an intercessor has many benefits. For example, I was at a prayer service leading prayer walking around praying, and all of a sudden, I started to see this lady's son who was in the service going inside a cop car, then I saw him coming out of the cop car. As I was praying, the Lord gave me the revelation of that vision, so I interceded on her son's behalf and told her what I saw concerning her son. She was puzzled about the vision and in denial at the same time. A month later, her son confessed to having trouble with the law. Several months later, the charges were dropped. Now can you see the power you have as a seer that is called into intercession? The majority of the time, if God is showing you a problem, this means he has given you the authority to make a change. So, my question to you is, will you use the authority given to you? Will you use your authority to make a change?

It is imperative to intercede, and we see that in Genesis, chapter 18. When Abraham interceded on behalf of his nephew Lot, it saved him and his daughters from a city of sin. This place was extremely contaminated by sexual perversion. It was so contaminated that God wanted the town destroyed. Abraham's intercession saved the lives of his loved ones. Being an Intercessor is more than a person praying for others or standing in the gap for a region, city, and state. Intercession is a form of intimacy. An Intercessors' first role is to have intimacy with the Father. Intimacy is said so often, but saying it slow I hear, into him, you see. The more time you spend in his presence, the more he will reveal to you. Being an Intercessor is a great job. As men and women of God, we should participate in intercession as much as possible.

Being a seer has benefits, reaching dimensions of intercession you have never seen before. You must get to a point where you desire to go higher. We should never be in the same place of interceding; everything in God must grow. In the Bible, Jesus cursed the fig tree for not growing. Intercessor, I encourage you, do not just exist; level up. "But grow in grace, and in the knowledge of our Lord and Savior Jesus Christ. To him be glory both now and forever. Amen." 2 Peter 3:18 KJV. As a seer/Intercessor, 'love what you do and do what you love. It is the passionate, heartfelt prayer of the righteous that gets results (James 5:16). Intercession is a lifestyle; the best part is you are partnered with the best to do it. The Holy Spirit will guide you and prepare you for every level you are in. (Romans 8:26) I want to encourage you as an Intercessor through a testimony. This vision required a length of time and patience. I believe this will stir you as it is stirring me as I am writing it down. In the spring of 2019, my wife and I were fasting concerning the next move for us as a family. Every day we prayed at noon and were praying and interceding for our family, children, finances, etc. The presence of God was so intense my stomach began hurting. The rivers of living water were flowing. As the encounter with God took place, my spiritual eyes opened, and I started to see what he had for my family and me. I was in awe until the last vision he showed me. I was so shocked and in disbelief at what I saw. I paused for a moment, and my silence caught my wife's attention. My wife asked me what is wrong, and me being fearful of that vision, I started weeping. I then told her the vision was that my three children's mother was lying in a casket. This vision was so vivid that even a new Intercessor would know this was from God. The Holy Spirit told me I gave you the vision to stop it from happening. My wife and I immediately began interceding on her behalf, binding and breaking every assignment of hell until we felt a shift. Fast-forward to the spring of 2020; the world was in a pandemic, and Coronavirus viciously claimed thousands of lives.

I received a phone call that my children's mother was on her deathbed due to Coronavirus. I immediately went into deep intercession, then a couple of days later, the Lord reminded me about the vision I had the year prior. The reminder put me at ease. The same week she called me and said, "Sean, I thank God for your prayers because I was leaving this earth," wow! The benefits of being a seer/Intercessor changes things. This changed my life, so I pray that it will change your life as well. It made me a forever lover of intercession and committed to trusting what I see. Great men and women of God, I urge you to accept who you are and pray what you see.

About the author

Sean Hunter is a co- founder of Hunter Ministries. He's a husband, a father of four beautiful children and an emerging Prophet. He attended Wood House Bible School in Bronx New York we're he obtained multiple certificates from the teaching's of spiritual warfare, The book of Acts, and general Bible. Sean has a passion for deliverance, prophetic, and the supernatural. Sean's missions to reach the lost by the unique and radical way he delivers the gospel.

Contact Info:

Email: seanhunter516@yahoo.com

https://www.facebook.com/HuntersMinistries

6

Mantled for the Assignment

By Tammy Lawrence

Some of us have been not only called but also chosen from the womb to fight, when you were birthed from powerful Seers who've had to war their entire lives. Now here you are, a breached birth fighting from the womb to live so that you can complete a major assignment in the earth realm. You then finally realize just how real the mantle truly is. Hearing stories from my parents of the warfare they went through even to get me out of the womb alive allows me to see why I've been chosen as a Prophetic Seer with an Apostolic Priestly assignment in the Earth realm for such a time as this. It amazes me of the opposition that I would encounter continually until I realized who God had called me to be, and the oil that I had been graced with that manifested even while in the womb. I am thankful and honored to have been chosen, handpicked, and mandated by Almighty God to be a part of His strategic plan and purpose in this hour. It's been an honor to have had some very anointed teachers and mentors that have been key to my process. Coming out of the Holy Spirit school has taken me to a whole new realm of victory and power—growing as an intercessor while learning to hear the voice of God. It has been essential to my everyday life and has landed me in an assignment that I couldn't get out of if I tried. But now, coming to understand why and how I see in the realms of the spirit and the power that flows from on high is amazing. Walking with the Holy Spirit is priceless, and I wouldn't trade it for the world.

As a Prophetic Intercessor, you're not just called to pray but to stand in the gap and pray according to the leading of the Holy Spirit for people, places, and things in agreement with His heart. As you pray, having the revelator's Seer eyes, you are shown hidden mysteries to guide your prayers from a deeper dimension.

Sometimes revelations can also come to you through visions, dreams, or open visions while you are wide awake. When you are mantled as a true Seer, God will show you things because He knows that He can trust you to pray and intercede in the matter. This is a great mandate and not to be taken lightly in any way. God's Prophetic Seers and Intercessors are chosen by Almighty God to intervene, interrupt, and intercept the enemy's plans as His representatives in the earth realm. This is a powerful assignment to be called to, and if you're graced to have been chosen for the task, you must know that it is to be handled with honor and care. The Holy Spirit will teach you how to move and flow strategically with Him and how NOT to grieve Him by moving before the time or speaking prematurely what

He shows you. Always see more than you say until it's time to release unless it's just for you to pray over and not share at all. Everything given to you by the Holy Spirit is not for speaking everywhere or to everybody, especially out of season. Carrying more than one mantle is tough, and it must be cultivated properly so that you move in accuracy and precision on all accounts. I can remember once when I was waiting to go into a prophetic conference while I stood under the tent waiting for the line to move, the Holy Spirit said to me, "you can read while you wait," and so I thought, "oh ok." I prayed over my bible and opened it, it opened to Luke 7:22-28, where Jesus was doing many signs, wonders, and miracles, as the disciples of John questioned Him. Jesus responded, *"then Jesus answering said unto them, Go your way, and tell John what things ye have seen and heard; how that the blind see, the lame walk, the lepers are cleansed, the deaf hear, the dead are raised, to the poor the gospel is preached."* Then Jesus asked the people a powerful question, which I think He was alluding to me as well. The question shocked me and was this, "*What went ye out into the wilderness for to see?*" In this, He asked and then gave answers, but then asked three times, so as I looked around I saw many things like the reeds (trees) shaken by the wind as the wind blew, and many who were clothed in soft garments, ready to go inside and hear a Prophet speak. On the last time Jesus asked this question, the Holy Spirit prompted me to look around again. "*But what went ye out for to see? A prophet? Yea, I say unto you, and much more than a prophet." This is he, of whom it is written, Behold, I send my messenger before thy face, which shall prepare thy way before thee. For I say unto you, among those that are born of women there is not a greater prophet than John the Baptist: but he that is least in the kingdom of God is greater than he."* Wow!

Coming out of that encounter, I was totally blown away, the Lord was saying to me; "you are going to see and hear a Prophet, but you're much more than a Prophet yourself." I was in total amazement, and when they called me to come up to the front to go inside, I could barely stand because the power of the Holy Ghost had completely engulfed me, and my spiritual sister told me that I was glowing. I'm here to tell you today that you have a divine call and destiny that's been chosen by Almighty God for you to fulfill. The call and assignment on your life are great though you may not even understand it in its totality at this time. Nevertheless, you are special to God. I love how Jesus asked about seeing. In other words, that Seer in you has been authorized with signs, wonders, and miracles following. He asked, "what did you go out to see?" You've been called to see some things on a higher dimension than you could even imagine. That Seer gift in you is calling you to see in the natural realm and the supernatural realm. I believe Jesus knew what they were looking at naturally, but He was activating a more profound anointing on top of that Prophetic gifting. He revealed to the disciples that there was a Seer in them and that the miracles that He was performing that they would do so much more. The revelator was revealing to the disciples the anointing that they were about to walk in.

The Seer can see not just on a low level but on a much higher supernatural dimension. When you carry the anointing as Seer, things are revealed to you that many others may not see or even understand. You walk in supernatural divine revelations and can tap into mysteries from on high. This is a powerful oil to be entrusted with because it not only reveals things to you but allows you to see the enemy's schemes, plots, and tactics beforehand. That Seer in you is a threat to the kingdom of darkness and is accompanied by the eagle eye of the revelator to keep you on point so that you can intercede without fail. The revelator's eye sees through the eyes of the spirit and is equipped to counterattack and hit bulls' eye on target every single time. Since you're much more than a Prophet, you've been called as an Intercessor, Seer, and Revealer of prophetic secrets that are given by divine grace. This is super powerful and must be strengthened continuously through spending quality time alone with God. The role of the Intercessor is to pray without ceasing and is much deeper than that of a regular prayer life. We come to go between and among and to stand in the gap by the leading of the Holy Spirit for people, places, and things that are precious to God. Being mantled for the assignment allows you to do the works as Jesus did and greater. I encourage you today to embrace this calling but nurture, cultivate, and sharpen this gifting, knowing that you are bonafide and powerful in God. Oh, what a mighty, true, and unique position to walk in. Don't lose heart in the rough places but know that you're not alone; you have help, know that this oil is costly, so carry it well; as you wear the mantle with grace, you will complete the assignment unto the very end.

About the Author

Prophetess Tammy Lawrence is an authentic Prophetic Seer, Intercessor, published author, entrepreneur, and anointed vessel for the Kingdom of God. She flows strongly in the supernatural and mentors many others to walk out their fullest potential while embracing their God-given mandate. Prophetess engages in outreach ministry with a strong focus on the restoration and healing of God's people globally.

Contact Info:

Facebook: Tammy Lawrence

Instagram: Prophetess Tammy Lawrence

7

Seer Look Up

By Yeleina Morgan

"See, I have this day set thee over the nations and over the kingdoms, to root out, and to pull down, and to destroy, and to throw down, to build, and to plant."

Jeremiah 1:10

When one thinks about the ability to see, the standard definition of what we know as sight or eyesight comes to mind. Sight, commonly defined as "the process, power, or function of seeing specifically: the physical sense by which light stimuli received by the eye are interpreted by the brain and constructed into a representation of the position, shape, brightness, and usually color of objects in space: mental or spiritual perception."[1] Our eyesight is one of our most essential senses, especially when we understand that "80% of what we perceive comes through our sense of sight."[2] But every believer has two sets of eyes, our physical eyes, with which we view the physical world around us and our spiritual eyes that keenly perceive and discern spiritual truths.

In the Old Testament, two words primarily to refer to a Seer: ra'ah and chozeh. Ra'ah means "to see," particularly in the sense of seeing visions. Other meanings include "to gaze," "to look upon," and "to perceive." Chozeh means, "a beholder in vision," and can also be translated to mean "gazer" or "stargazer." When it comes to prophetic revelation, a Prophet is one who is a divinely inspired hearer, and then speaks the word of God in a spontaneous, bubbling forth flow that starts out in the womb of their belly and begins to fill them up until it flows out of their mouths, and they speak the utterance, while a Seer is one who sees with spiritual eyes; perceive the message of God with their inner eye, receive the meaning of that which seems obscure to others; therefore is an interpreter and clarifier of eternal truth. Seers, by the power of the Lord operating through them, foresee the future from both the past and the present.

The difference between a Prophet and a Seer's purpose is that while they are both sent to reveal the wonders of Christ and God's purpose for a generation, and while true Seers are Prophets, not all Prophets are Seers. Joel 2:28 declares that "And it shall come to pass afterward, that I will pour out my spirit upon all flesh; and your sons and your daughters shall prophesy, your old men shall dream dreams, your young men shall see visions." The Seer is usually more visionary than auditory and rather than receiving words that they attempt to repeat or flow with; Seers often see pictures, open visions, or dreams that they then describe. They have prophetic insight, foresight, hindsight, and oversight which they used to onfirm the directions God has given as they look beyond the physical dimension and peer into spiritual realms and dimensions to reveal God's word and ways to awaken people to God and His sovereignty.

Seers have the ability to see God's original intention. When they see something that is not spiritually in line, they call for alignment and resolution of spiritual issues because they discern more than the problem and God's original intention regarding a situation. There are many instances in Biblical history where we are shown those who operated as Seers are often mentioned. For example, 1 Samuel 9 records, "When a man went to inquire of God, he said, 'Come, let us go to the Seer,' and in fact, Samuel was called a Seer several times.

Through prophetic dreaming, God can communicate directions that one might not hear while awake or going forth in day to day activities. Why, then, should God be limited to using only ears to communicate with us? Did He not also give four other senses with which to experience Him? He can speak through touch, taste, smell, and, most certainly, sight.

God created light so that we would See. Genesis 1:31 says, "Then God saw everything that He had made, and indeed it was very good." Every time God created 'he saw that it was good.' In Genesis 1:29, God said to Adam, 'See what I have created for you'; God's perspective is not ours ... but He gives Seers' access to His perspective; "And He said, Hear now my words: If there be a prophet among you, I the LORD will make myself known unto him in a vision, and will speak unto him in a dream." Numbers 12:6

There is a difference between seeing and looking. When we focus on something, we begin to connect with it, so 'seeing' occurs when something happens to a person; looking is the action that someone takes even before seeing a thing. In our relationship with God, it is critical that we see what God is doing. To be sensitive to God's thoughts and plans and to discern with our spiritual senses so that "the eyes of your understanding will become enlightened." In Ephesians 1:18 God is continually calling His Seer's to see beyond and to "open our eyes to see the wonderful truths in His law," Psalms 119:18

The Seer anointing is a gift and anointing that is to be taken purposefully and soberly. It is a weighty assignment. When we are discerning both good and evil, we need to remember there is a purpose for it. It is for us to bring forth God's desires, plans, and strategies into our realm of authority and influence. We are created in the image of God, and "Greater is He that is in me then he that is in the world," 1 John 4:4. Jesus said, "We would do Greater works than He did," John 14:12.

Seer, you are God's dreamer! When you see something, you know what you are supposed to do. You are a visionary filled with faith. You see destiny and will strategize with the Lord to bring destiny to manifestation. God is raising you within this generation of those whom He can trust with His secrets; a company of Seers and prophetic voices that will emerge with the ability to bring understanding and revelation to His mysteries. He is calling forth those willing to penetrate beyond the veil, seeing with sharpness and clarity into spiritual realms and dimensions. You are called to move out of this natural, limited mindset and move into Christ-consciousness. You have to realize that you can see and hear with your spiritual eyes and ears much further than you can in the natural. Look beyond Seer, what wondrous things do you behold?

References

1 - Merriam-webster.com. Definition Of SIGHT. https://www.merriam-webster.com/dictionary/sight

2 - Medical Eye Center | Importance of Eye Care | Medford.

https://www.medicaleyecenter.com/2016/06/20/importance-eye-care/

About the author

Yeleina Morgan, a native New Yorker, a graduate of Regent University with an Associate Degree in Biblical Studies is a published author of "From Spiritual Disability to Spiritual Maturity" and a Co-author of The Role of AnIntercessor Vol I, II and III. Yeleina is a catalyst who ignites andmotivates others to achieve their dreams.

Contact Info:

Email: Yeleinamorgan@gmail.com

Facebook.com/yeleinamorgan716

8

The Birther Within

By Wanda Gentry

The very first thing or assignment I have is to remind you of who you are, the potential you possess on the inside of you as well as the greatness that is about to be revealed through you by the power of God. ***1.*** Know that you are: ***Anointed***, ***Chosen***, ***Equipped***, ***Qualified*** for the JOB (whatever God has called you to do & whatever you put your hands to. **2.** You carry the

Spirit of your heavenly Father, you are more than a ***Conqueror***, you are a ***LifeSaver***, there is a ***Warrior*** on the inside of you. **3.** You have Kingdom ***Vision***, ***Creativity***, ***Passion*** and ***Discernment***. **Most Importantly I want you to know that you are **LOVED by God**!!*

You are who God says you are......

You can do what God says you can do....

You will not return unto him void....

You will accomplish everything He has sent you out to do....

You will prosper (flourish, thrive, grow, succeed) where unto the things, places and people He has sent you.....

In Jesus Name!!

Amen

The Past

I must first tell you of where we were in order for you to appreciate where we are going or embarking on. In the past we as Christians, Saints or Children of God felt that we had to have something tangible to prove or validate that were/are blessed and that the hand of God IS upon our lives. It varied from but not limited to a spouse, certain jobs, big house, nice car, our children, money/ finances, connections. Without any tangible or visible signs of any of these many of us felt like God was not good to us, we were not blessed or something was wrong. The canon of scripture found in ***Matthew 6:33 (KJV)*** – says, "But ***seek ye first*** the kingdom of God, and his righteousness; and all these **things shall be added** unto you.

If the truth be told, many of us can find ourselves in one of the following categories: We sought after things more than the kingdom, we sought things and the kingdom; desiring them both equally. If you noticed the Word of God said, "**Seek** Ye First ***The Kingdom***" and "***Things shall be added***" not "***Seek*** The

Kingdom" and"***Seek*** and things shall be added". *(As a people we were busy seeking things and trying to birth things).* Do not get me wrong God wants us to have things. I am just stating God is a God of order. In the canon of scripture, Matthew clearly states that the order in which God wants us to do things according to the Kingdom.

God said in His word that he would give us the desires of our heart, Psalm 37:4. Remember it is his good pleasure to give us the Kingdom. He died that we might have life and have it more abundantly!

"***He wants us to have things; but he doesn't want things to have us"***

Let me repeat it! God wants us to have things; but He does not want things to have us.

Shall – It means will or intend to, and it also expresses duty or moral obligation. It is in the second and third persons, that *shall* implies a promise, command or determination. The word *shall* appears 7587 times in the Bible. Whenever you see the word "*shall*" in the

Bible it is tied or attached to a promise from God. Example, Ye *shall* receive power…, Seek and ye *shall* find….

God is bound by His Word. Meaning, God keeps His promises. **Numbers 23:19 (KJV) 19** "God is not a man, that he should lie; neither the son of man, that he should repent: hath he said, and shall he not do it? or hath he spoken, and shall he not make it good?"

2 Corinthians 1:20 – (KJV)

20 "For all the promises of God in him are yea, and in him Amen, unto the glory of God by us."

Present

I really want us to finish this year (2020) strong going into the new year (2021). Not just having the right posture, words (mouth - what we say and speak) lined up, but our hearts and thought life as well. Let us just go ahead and kill, tear-down, uproot the lies of the enemy that you will never amount to anything, that you don't have what it takes, you will always be broke, that lack, poverty and not enough shall be your portion. LISTEN!! I thank God we are now in a place of maturity and we are no longer falling for his tactics. God has raised up an army, a generation of people who are not afraid, will not compromise, are ready, and well equipped to advance the kingdom in ways we have never imagined. God is getting ready to blow our minds! We have heard and many of us sing the song "Blow My Mind". Are we really ready to see, experience and walk in the obedience necessary for God to usher in and carry out His latter-day glory in the earth? I am here to tell you whether you are ready or not; "Watch Out", HERE IT COMES!! Better yet "IT ALREADY IS!" Somebody shout Hallelujah!

Future

No longer will we be held captive, bound, hoodwinked, or bamboozled by the tricks and lies of the enemy. We have moved out of the place of being in years of manipulation, bondage and captivity. God has set us free, therefore, we are free indeed, liberated and made whole. The old man has died and there is no more struggle and people shall see the eternal workings of God being made manifested in us (man) in the earth. There are some doors God is closing and things He is putting an end to now, because it has been going on way too long and God said enough is enough. There are also things God is about to birth forth in the earth, and he is sending out the clarion call for us to get in place and in position. What is about to be birthed forth is not like anything else that has ever been done or seen before. There are going to be those who will walk in a supernatural grace of God. You will see the power and presence of God all over them. Many have their eyes on the virus, deaths, murders, violence, and injustice. None of this can compare to what God is doing and getting ready to do. I want to encourage you to keep your trust, hope, faith, and eyes on God. The God we serve is ALL POWERFUL, there is NO ONE else like Him, nor anything greater than Him. He is about to reveal Himself as Lord God Almighty. **Exodus 14:14 (NIV)** – "The LORD will fight for you; you need only to be still."

The (NLT) – says, “just stay calm” and the (KJV) says, - “and ye shall hold your peace.” **Joshua 23:10 (GNT)** – “Any one of you can make a thousand men run away, because the LORD your God is fighting for you, just as he promised.”

“***In Order to Birth The New; The Old Must Die!***

The Law of Physics states - “two objects of matter cannot occupy the same space at the same time.” ***The Word of God*** declares – “where there is light, darkness cannot stay. Either you will choose to be children of the light and walk in the light, or you are going to walk in darkness. You cannot do both. You must be one or the other, just like either you are hot or cold in Revelations 3:16 (KJV) – “So then because thou art lukewarm, and neither cold nor hot, I will spue thee out of my mouth” The New King James Version says, “VOMIT!” wow... The word of God also says Genesis 8:22 (KJV) While earth remaineth, seedtime and harvest, and cold and heat, and summer and winter, and day and night shall not cease.

In Order for God to birth the new, the old must die or be done away with. This seems like a very bold, cruel or harsh pill to swallow; but it is true, andt is something that we have to stop ignoring, deal with, and not keep brushing under the rug. Many of us including myself have gone through a lot of hurt, pain, hard times, and struggles that we must get over, move past and move forward. We have been in a place called stuck or "Lodebar" for years, decades, centuries (generational curses and cycles). All jealousy, negativity, envy, strife, pettiness, backbiting, unforgiveness it all *HAS TO GO*!! The reason we are not as far along as we should be is we have those that are still pushing others to do the wrong things, saying the wrong things instead of pulling them over into *UNITY* and the Kingdom way of operating, and doing things. Time to come out, separate ourselves, *BE Delivered*, *BE Free* and ***NEVER LOOK BACK!***

The Meat of The Matter

Let us get to the meat of the matter. Life as some of us knew it is GONE! I don't know if you noticed it but in the spiritual realm the pace has picked up. The race now must not only be ran with patience, but also with haste. Done quickly but not ***haphazardly*** *(lacking and obvious principles of organization or thought put into it).* For many of us, our hearts, minds and posture have changed. The focus has been shifted from off us and put back on God. *Our* hearts and mindsets have gone through a reset or recalibration to where we are no longer focused on a "material world" or storing up (temporal) treasures here on earth. We have traded it for a "Kingdom Mindset" that is focused on (eternal) treasures in heavenly places, leaving an inheritance for our children and their children's children and the birthing forth of the Kingdom of God, the will of the Father being done in the earth and God getting the glory! **Our hearts are now being turned back to the heart of God.*

The Changing of The Guards

The Changing of the Guard is a terminology we all are familiar with. Because of where we are spiritually and where we are going; God is concerned even the more about the spiritual well-being of His people. There are too many that are still in recovery from past wounds and hurts, too many still ***unstable (not – fit mentally for war)***, too many ***malnourished (not enough word)*** and too many ***unlearned (not trained or equipped for battle yet alone warfare).***

Therefore, God is sending ***reinforcements*** and raising up ***replacements*** to fill in where others have left off or left unfinished. Why? There is such an exchange, in-filling, transformation and weight of glory that God wants to release upon His people and in the earth realm as we prepare and draw nigh to the coming of Christ, "The Bridegroom" and "Soon Coming King". Therefore it is imperative that we detox, take off our former clothes (the old man/you), allow God to wash us, purge us, revive us again and transform us so that we may put on new garments as we prepare and await His arrival. God is not going to just patch us up, nor is He wanting to restore us. Although He can restore, He would rather make us "***Anew***". I am not saying God is going to stop restoring His people, but what I am saying is this. When you restore, refurbish, renovate something, all which are good, you are only bringing (returning), a thing or in this case a person back to his/her former condition or state. God *desires* to go way beyond reestablishing us in the earth and reinstating us to our former glory. Anew means "again," "afresh," "once again". God wants to do it "ONCE AGAIN!" Meaning the same thing He did with Adam; He wants to do it again. It has already been designed (predestined) for us to walk in the same dominion and authority just as He called Adam to walk, but GREATER. What God called and how He called Adam to be and walk in was for him and the times that he was in. The same is going to be for us and what God is calling us to "Do" and "BE" will be according to the dominion, authority, and power necessary to function, operate and carry out the assignment for the times (dispensational period) we are living in.

The Replacements

The word replacement means a person or thing that takes the place of another. Another definition is someone or persons appointed to represent or act on behalf of another. In Greek, replacement is αντικατάσταση, which is basically carries the same meaning in Hebrew {תַחֲלִיף} which means -***substitute, alternate, ersatz – compensation***. Antonyms for ersatz are genuine, natural and real.

What the spirit of the Lord is trying to convey is, He is raising up and has equipped "***Surrogates***" who are genuine, natural, and real with your best interest at hand. As I was pondering on what the Spirit of the Lord was saying concerning His replacements I jotted down the word **relief**. God is bringing peace, joy and hope to those that are despondent (in low spirits from loss of hope or courage), discouraged (having lost confidence or enthusiasm), discontented (dissatisfied, especially with one's circumstances), and fearful (afraid, unwilling or reluctant to do something for fear of the consequences). Blow the trumpets in Zion and sound the alarm. God is getting ready to intervene on our behalf.

Midwife Intercessor

Before I get started I want you to know that there are both midwives naturally and spiritually. The Hebrew term translated "the **Midwife**" (hameyaledet) may literally be translated "the childbirth assisting woman." Here are three references in the Bible where you can find the term {midwife}, they are Exodus 1:16, Genesis 35:17, and Genesis 38:28. The word derives from Old English Mid, "with" and wife "woman" thus meaning "with-woman", that is the person who is with the woman (mother) at childbirth. The word refers to midwives of either gender.

There is another term in the natural called "***doula.***" Doula (dou-la) is a woman, typically without formal obstetric training, who is employed to provide guidance and support to a pregnant woman during labor. He or She is a person employed to provide guidance and support to the mother of a newborn baby. In other words, spiritually God is sending or giving us not only Pastors after our own heart but Midwives and Caretakers (***doulas***) assigned to us for the welfare of the Kingdom Assignment, He has commissioned (custom-made, handed over to) each of us Spiritually to Birth. Just as He entrusted the midwives with Jochebed and the safe keeping of Moses, when Pharaoh sent out a decree that all the male children be wiped out. What many of you are carrying is going to bring such a paradigm shift in the earth, that it is going to catapult God's people into a dimension we have never encountered before. The enemy has sent out an all-out satanic attack on God's people. He wants to kill what you are carrying on the inside of you. He also wants to shut your mouth and keep you from releasing and decreeing God's word for this generation. There are those He has equipped for such a time as this to prepare the people for the End-Time and what is coming next!

There Will Be No Ectopic Births

There are many of us whose pregnancy right now is ***ectopic***, meaning (naturally) the baby we are carrying is in an abnormal place or position. It is a pregnancy in which the fertilized egg implants outside the uterus. The fertilized egg cannot survive outside the uterus therefore if left to grow, it may damage nearby organs and cause life-threatening loss of blood. Spiritually our baby is not fully aligned with what God wants to birth in us, we are also not where we need to be, therefore, our baby is not in the right position, fully nourished, developed nor ready to be delivered when it should. If delivered it can also cause our spiritual baby not to be able to function properly or survive. There are many of us that are behind schedule and others are "overdue." This is another reason why the replacements of surrogate-midwives, intercessors and vanguards are so important. Because the ones God is raising up have been proven faithful and obedient, God is adding (entrusting) them with more. This is not going to be an easy task, and I ask that if you are one of the ones God has chosen please take this very seriously. Remember to whom much is given, much is required. There is a heavy penalty for disobedience.

What Are We Birthing?

Now that I told you "why" we are birthing and the importance of what we are birthing, It would be of less effect or lacking if I didn't tell you the "what". The first thing again I want to reiterate is what we intercessors, vanguards, midwives and caregivers are birthing is NOTHING like the old. Those chosen have been impregnated with a greater weight, impartation, vision, anointing and glory of God. This grace or anointing carries not only the ability to effectively lead God's people, we are capable, and well-able to effectively deliver, then usher His people into position to be a part of the wedding party (chamber). If you've noticed those that have been chosen to be a part have to be in-line or aligned with what the bride or groom has set in place. There is a dress requirement and certain criteria for all those that take part spiritually as well. Jesus is coming back for a church without spot or wrinkle. Therefore the intercessors, midwives, and vanguard have died to the flesh and are no longer operating according to their flesh. They are not causing confusion, but UNITY and ushering in the peace of God in the midst of all this chaos and discord. They are walking and ushering in holiness, righteousness, turning the hearts of man back to the heart of God, back to the basics and foundational truths in the word of God. Most importantly the "Mind, Will, and Purpose of God." There are more in depth things that are going on behind the scenes in the spiritual realm. The purpose of this is to let you know how vitally important you are and what you are carrying is to God and the Kingdom.

"You Have People That Are Assigned or Attached To You"

The midwives in Exodus had Moses attached to their assignment. Remember, *you have people that are assigned or attached to you.* I bet you they never thought that they would be used to birth someone or something (a mighty move of God) or a "Movement."

"God Doesn't Always Reveal His Plans To Us"

God does not always reveal His plans to us, until the right time (His timing) when you are able to bear it without aborting or questioning it! You may have felt you were unimportant or insignificant, it may seem like what you were carrying was never going to take place. Listen!! Now is YOUR TIME! You are right at the brink! Do not give up now, do not turn around, run or retreat. PUSH!!! Instead, I tell you to bare down, keep your feet in the stirrups. PUSH!! PUSH!! PUSH!!! IT'S BIRTHING TIME.

Wanda Gentry,

#StayTrueToTheCall

#4EverEvolving

About the author

Wanda serves as an Associate Pastor and Intercessor under the leadership of Senior Pastor, Apostle Dr. Janice F. Thomas and Prophet/ Overseer Bishop Randall K. Thomas of His Kingdom Ministries located in Durham, NC. Pastor Wanda Gentry is founder of Kingdom Builder International Outreach Ministries and the author of The Enemies of Your Faith and The Role of an Intercessor Vol II and Vol III. Wanda's passion is to turn the heart of man back to the heart of God and help others become whole in Christ through teaching the holistic Gospel of Jesus Christ with simplicity, power and demonstration.

Contact Info:

Website: w: www.4everevolving.org

https://www.facebook.com/wanda.gentryivey

9

A Dreamer's Call To Prayer

By Crystal H. Moore

God has always dealt with me in ways that were different from what others around me experienced. I tend to hear, see, and feel things differently from others. I am called to pray at times when no one else around me wants to pray or even discerns what I'm being urged to pray. I know, I am called to the battlefield both day and night. I know, I have to be alert, attentive, and always ready. If you find yourself in the same or similar position, it simply means that you are an intercessor.

Although God deals with us all uniquely, He has always spoken to me through dreams and visions. As a little girl what I dreamt of at night would literally come to pass in the natural. I began to realize that I needed to pay attention to my dreams at a young age. At that time I did not have knowledge of the authority I had in the spiritual world. I also had not yet come into the knowledge of who I am in Christ or what my purpose for dreaming even was. Yet I knew there was something different about me.

I remember the first vision I had where I felt God was calling me to pray. I had a vision of heavenly angels warring on our behalf. The angels looked worn and appeared tired. There was an inner knowledge I had upon seeing the vision. I knew that the angels were weary from warfare and that we were not doing our part in praying. There was an urging in my spirit to pray. And so I began to pray. The more I prayed, the more I dreamed. The more I dreamed, the more I continued to pray. From this experience intercessory prayer was birthed in my life. I then understood that my dreams were showing me what I was to pray for. Now, almost

20 years later, I still see, hear, and discern what God wants me to pray for even more than before. However, this was not always my belief. I did not always believe in the power of prayer or intercession. There was a time in my life where I went through a period of traumatic events. As a result of those events I had a negative attitude towards God. I doubted what God could do through prayer. I felt that prayer was for the "super religious" and / or for the church mothers with the pocket full of candy. I did however believe that God was real. Yet I found myself at a young age needing the very thing I did not believe in.

I finally caved into putting prayer to work in my life when I was a teenager transitioning into college. My uncle and aunt, who were my caregivers, sat me down for a family talk. My uncle explained that they would not be providing any financial support for me to go to college. If I wanted to go to college I would have to figure it out on my own. I understood my family's position however, I had no clue what to do. I decided to put prayer to work in my life and petitioned God for help. It was my heart's desire to go to college. So I gathered as many college brochures and materials as I could and I decided that I was going to fast and pray. For three days while my aunt and uncle went to work, I laid across the living room floor on top of all the college brochures and I prayed. I cried out to God and I fasted. I genuinely asked God for help. On the turn of the third day I heard a still small voice say, "Barnard". I had never even heard of Barnard so I immediately opened my A-Z College Book and to my surprise there it was. Barnard College! I applied and was accepted into their HEOP (Higher Educational Opportunity Program) with 90% of my expenses paid. This included room and board, meal plan, tuition and books. I graduated in 1999 with a BA in Religion. I received four years worth of education totaling over 100k at no cost to me. I left Barnard owing a 10k loan which I was later able to have completely forgiven by teaching in an economically disadvantaged district. This experience proved to me that God is real and that prayer works. It showed me that fasting is effective when coupled with prayer. It motivated me to pray not only for myself but also for others. Intercession is not always easy. There have been times when I've discerned something to pray for and I did not pray for whatever reason. Most often it's a battle of the flesh that gets in the way when it is time to pray. As a result of not praying when I was prompted to, I have seen some disheartening things happen. When you realize you have missed the mark for whatever reason there can be extreme feelings of guilt and remorse. The enemy has a way of tormenting your thoughts when this happens and that is because he doesn't want you to pray. If he can get you to feel defeated then he can stop you from praying. The enemy doesn't want you to tap into your true role as an intercessor. He does not want you to know or operate in who you are. If this has happened to you, where you have "dropped the ball" in not praying or let flesh get in the way, do not live in condemnation. I had to let my experiences be hard learning lessons. We must learn from the experience and use it to step into our calling.

Remember, "There is therefore now no condemnation to them which are in Christ Jesus, who walk not after the flesh, but after the Spirit." Romans 8:1 KJV. Unfortunately, I have seen negative things come to pass that I dreamed about and failed to pray for. However, I have also witnessed many great things that have come to pass as a result of constant prayer and intercession. When it comes to prayer the Bible says in James 5:16 "Confess your faults one to another, and pray one for another, that ye may be healed. The effectual fervent prayer of a righteous man availeth much."

There is power in prayer. There are answers in prayer, and there are testimonies birthed through prayer. Maybe you find your story similar to my own in one way or another. Maybe you've also had some victories and defeats as an intercessor. Our challenge now is to be alert and focused during intercession. We must be intentional in our posture and intentional in our time spent with God. The role of an intercessor never stops. It is continual hour by hour, minute by minute. We must learn not to speak on everything we sense, discern, or that's disclosed in confidentiality. We have to be sure to treat others the way we want to be treated regarding matters of the heart. Our call is to study the word of God so we can pray the word of God as we intercede.

Now more than ever our intercessory prayer is needed. We are needed for our family, our friends, and the world at large. The list of what we are called to pray for can be excessive, and the warfare attached to what we are called to do is great. "For we wrestle not against flesh and blood, but against principalities, against powers, against the rulers of the darkness of this world, against spiritual wickedness in high places." Ephesians 6:12 KJV Although this is true, Luke 10:19 is also true.

"Behold, I give unto you power to tread on serpents and scorpions, and over all the power of the enemy: and nothing shall by any means hurt you." So take your rightful place as an intercessor. Realize that you were crafted and molded into who you are for a reason. Embrace your giftings and uniqueness in Him. Get back into position if you've lost your way. Know who and whose you are in the Kingdom of God. Yes there is warfare attached to intercession, but know and be assured that we are on the winning side!

About the author

Crystal H. Moore was born and raised in The Bronx, New York. She graduated from Barnard College with a BA in Religion and is currently an educator in Georgia. Crystal is a woman of many talents, but her greatest passion is encouraging others to be all that they can be in Christ.

Contact Info:

Email: crystalhmoore2@yahoo.com
Facebook: https://www.facebook.com/crystalhmoore2
Instagram: @simplycrystalsimplyme
Twitter: @Simplycrystals1
Youtube: SimplyCrystalsimplyme

www.ingramcontent.com/pod-product-compliance
Ingram Content Group UK Ltd.
Pitfield, Milton Keynes, MK11 3LW, UK
UKHW020138250726
13967UKWH00002B/741

9 781716 115608